Natural Evangelism

*STRATEGIES FOR ORDINARY
PEOPLE TO MAKE AN
EXTRAORDINARY DIFFERENCE*

Randy Lariscy

WordTruth Press
USA

© 2015 by Randy Lariscy.

All rights reserved. No part of this publication may be reproduced, stored in a retrieval system, or transmitted in any form or by any means – electronic, mechanical, photocopy, recording, or any other – except for brief quotations in printed reviews, without prior permission of the author.

Cover art provided courtesy of *Beautiful Events*.

All scripture quotations, unless otherwise indicated, are taken from the Holy Bible, New International Version®, NIV®. Copyright ©1973, 1978, 1984, 2011 by Biblica, Inc.™ Used by permission of Zondervan. All rights reserved worldwide. www.zondervan.com The "NIV" and "New International Version" are trademarks registered in the United States Patent and Trademark Office by Biblica, Inc.™

1st Edition, published by WordTruth Press, USA (SAN 920-2811).

ISBN: 978-0-9852899-8-0

Library of Congress Control Number: 2014916028

Additional books by Randy Lariscy

Heaven
Portraits of Forgiveness (2nd Ed.)
Speedy Devotions (Vol. 1) – Wise Choices
The Book of Mark (Vol. 1)

Foreword

My friend and co-laborer, Randy Lariscy, is the picture of a life on mission! The "mission" for Randy is seeing people come to a faith experience through the transforming power of Jesus Christ. Randy's strategy for evangelism is very simple and lasts for a lifetime!

Buy his book, Natural Evangelism, apply the principles, and then simply live a life of being salt and light to a very dark world. You will be blessed and be a blessing as well!

Dr. Dwight "Ike" Reighard
President/CEO, MUST Ministries
Senior Pastor, Piedmont Church

Acknowledgements

To Dr. Victor Benavides:

He is the evangelist's evangelist. He could share the gospel with a brick and the whole wall would get saved. He is amazing. Even more amazing is the fact that he took the time to personally teach me when I was unable to attend any classes on a regular basis. One of my children had serious health problems that kept my wife and I on a tag-team to care for him. But Victor cared enough to take me through the lessons as I was able – an hour here and there. It took six months but I learned how to share the good news of Jesus Christ. Thank you Victor - your passion and energy helped to light an evangelism fire that continues to burn brightly.

To my "mighty warriors" (2 Sam. 23:8, NIV)

Many thanks to Jeff, Marshall, Cameron, and David for your editing contributions. You encourage and challenge me daily.

Contents

An Unlikely Book   15

A Natural Outcome   23

  ❖ *Uniquely You in Christ*   24
  ❖ *The Five REACH Strategies*   26

Relating in Love   31

  ❖ *The Gospel is Personal*   34
  ❖ *Leverage Your Life Zones*   36
  ❖ *Practice Unconditional Love*   41
  ❖ *Use Your Unique Personality*   44

Exploring the Spiritual Journey   49

  ❖ *The Gospel Requires Words*   51
  ❖ *Everyone is on a Spiritual Journey*   53
  ❖ *Starting the Conversation*   58
  ❖ *Understanding their condition*   63
  ❖ *Sharing the good news*   65

Asking People to the Party   75

- ❖ *Come and See*   77
- ❖ *Small Groups Have a Big Impact*   79
- ❖ *A Community Connection*   82

Communicating the Positive   87

- ❖ *Your Worldview Matters*   88
- ❖ *Your Future is Bright*   89
- ❖ *Your Speech Should Be Bright*   90
- ❖ *Be Positive but Real*   93
- ❖ *Connect the Dots of Faith*   96

Helping in Tangible Ways   103

- ❖ *Jesus Modeled Community Service*   105
- ❖ *Compassion Drives Outreach*   108
- ❖ *Plan Meaningful Involvement*   111
- ❖ *Credibility Drives Relationships*   116

Implementing the REACH Strategies   123

Appendix A – The GRACE Outline   129

- ❖ *The GRACE Outline*   130
- ❖ *Closing Points*   136

About the Author   139

An Unlikely Book

Natural Evangelism is a concept that, frankly, feels foreign to me. As a natural introvert, striking up a conversation with people is just plain hard. *"What should I say, how should I begin, what if I flub up my words?"* These are the thoughts that blaze through my mind as I struggle uncomfortably with people. How then did I reach the point of being able to write a book on personal evangelism?

In short, I, like you, am on a journey in following Jesus.

This journey is a process of getting to know our Savior, understanding His way of thinking and living, and becoming *(a key word since it is never a completed task in this life)* obedient to Him. The more I get to know Jesus, the greater He becomes and the less I see myself being very

Natural Evangelism

much like Him. But the more I get to know Jesus, the more effective I become in His kingdom work. I try to walk in His ways as best I understand Him. And you should as well for in that journey, He changes us.

> HE MUST BECOME GREATER; I MUST BECOME LESS.
> (JOHN 3:30, NIV)

Understand that an introvert is not one who necessarily dislikes being around people. I like being around people. Yes, large crowds make me a bit self-conscious but I still enjoy settings with lots of people. The key difference between an extrovert and an introvert is that an extrovert is *energized* around other people while an introvert is *drained*. As an introvert, I must have alone time to recharge my batteries after being around people. But I still like people. The other distinction of introverts is in the ease of striking up friendships with new people. It seems to come natural to extroverts but is exceedingly hard for me.

Evangelism has always seemed to be a scary proposition since it involved knocking on the doors of strangers with the intent of sharing the gospel *(so I was told)*. Yet in order to be faithful to the LORD *(so I thought)*, I forced myself to get trained in evangelism. There was the memorization of an outline – the approach I learned involved the world's longest gospel presentation, a roughly 20-minute detailed outline. I learned to go into neighborhoods and knock on a stranger's door and quickly lead them to diagnostic questions that would provide a segue into the comprehensive gospel presentation. There were times that this method resulted in a conversion – someone would actually pray to receive Jesus Christ as LORD and Savior in front of a total stranger. It was certainly not the norm but it happened.

Natural Evangelism

And it happened often enough to keep me going – getting out of my comfort zone and doing the hard work of evangelism.

Over the years, I came to a startling conclusion: what I was doing was not natural. Jesus commanded us to make disciples as a lifestyle.[1] I know also that Jesus formed me in the womb (Isa. 49:5; Jer. 1:5) and made me with a unique design (Psa. 139:13:16; Eph. 2:10). Perhaps the confrontational approach is natural for some of His people. I submit that it is not natural for *most* people. It is certainly not natural for me.

So I began a study in evangelism in the New Testament to test this conclusion. Here is what I found:

---

1 This key to the Great Commission in Matthew 28:19-20 is the phrase "Go, therefore, and make disciples" (HCSB) translates from the Greek a verb that is in the present tense, indicating continuous action – hence, a lifestyle. You might translate it "As you go .... make disciples..."

- Some instances of apostles and disciples preaching the gospel to large crowds – in the synagogues and coliseums.

- Many instances of apostles and disciples and *ordinary* believers talking to people they met along the way, in the highways and byways of life.

Evangelism should be as natural as breathing. So let's define it this way:

> NATURAL EVANGELISM IS A LIFESTYLE OF SHARING THE LOVE AND MESSAGE OF CHRIST IN THE CONTEXT OF RELATIONSHIPS YOU FORM ALONG THE WAY.

This takes so much pressure off of the whole idea of evangelism for me. I hope you will find it easier to breathe with this understanding. You are not expected to preach the gospel to crowds or parse deep theological questions. Nor are you expected to confront every person you see with the four spiritual laws. You are expected to love people and, in the course of your relationships, help them along in their spiritual journey with the gospel – the good news of Jesus Christ.

Join me as we discover a natural approach to evangelism that both extroverts and introverts alike can utilize to reach people for Christ.

For His kingdom,

Randy Lariscy

A Natural Outcome

NATURAL EVANGELISM IS A NATURAL
OUTCOME OF FOLLOWING JESUS.

It is not the intent of this book to turn you into a *gospel gunslinger*. Some authors are so bent on pumping you up for evangelism that they create the unrealistic expectation that you can win every person you meet to Christ - in five minutes or less. People quickly become disillusioned, believing there is something wrong with them rather than the evangelism approach they learned from the evangelism guru.

The goal of winning people to Christ is noble and biblical.[2] The method, however, must be

---

[2] *Those who are wise will shine like the brightness of the heavens, and those who lead many to righteousness, like the stars for ever and ever. (Daniel 12:3, NIV)*

tailored to you as an individual so that it is a natural part of your life. The same is true for the people you meet – the method must be tailored to the unique culture in which you live.

❖ Uniquely You in Christ

In order to raise a child to become a productive, responsible adult, the Bible explains that you should:

> TRAIN UP A CHILD IN THE WAY HE SHOULD GO, AND WHEN HE IS OLD HE WILL NOT DEPART FROM IT. (PROV. 22:6, NKJV)

The way *"he should go"* indicates that training should be specific to the individual child. A child that is naturally inquisitive learns best when given the opportunity to explore rather than listening to endless lectures. A child that has no desire for sports becomes frustrated and angry when forced to compete on the ball field. One must understand the natural designs of children to successfully raise them to adulthood.

Jesus invites you to follow Him in a personal, loving relationship that lasts for time and eternity. The natural outcome of following Jesus is that He will make you successful in reaching people with the good news. His command is very simple:

> FOLLOW ME, AND I WILL MAKE YOU FISHERS OF MEN. (MATTHEW 4:19, NKJV)

Your job is to follow the LORD Jesus. His job is to train you in reaching people with the good news. And you can be sure that Jesus knows you inside and out. He is the One who designed you. Who better to mold you into a soul-winner based on your unique personality, gifts, and life experience?

This also takes all the pressure off of you when it comes to learning evangelism. Jesus is responsible for molding you into a disciple-maker. You are responsible for drawing close to Him and responding obediently to His direction.

❖ The Five REACH Strategies

In the following chapters we will explore five natural strategies that will help you reach your friends and family with the life-changing message of Jesus. These are long-term, life-long activities that will accomplish several critical goals for you as a follower of Christ and for the growth of the church of Jesus Christ:

- Develop prospects for the kingdom of God.

- Create opportunities to share the good news about Jesus.
- See people come to faith in the LORD Jesus.

These five strategies are not sequential – they each stand alone and you can start with any of them. But they all work together over time to accomplish the goal of giving your message a context of love and credibility that is vital to the success of the gospel.

The acrostic REACH will be used to represent these five strategies:

- R stands for Relating
- E stands for Exploring
- A stands for Asking
- C stands for Communicating
- H stands for Helping

Natural Evangelism

As you read each chapter, make it a goal to practice what you learn that week. Find a trusted Christian friend to share what you have learned and get their advice on ways to be more effective in that area. As the Bible tells us:

> TWO ARE BETTER THAN ONE, BECAUSE THEY
> HAVE A GOOD RETURN FOR THEIR LABOR:
> IF EITHER OF THEM FALLS DOWN,
> ONE CAN HELP THE OTHER UP.
> (ECCL. 4:9-10, NIV)

You are beginning a new stage in your journey with the LORD Jesus. Your sincerity in following Christ, your desire to see people come to faith in Him, and your faithfulness in getting equipped will no doubt result in a great harvest for the kingdom of God. What great joy there is in Heaven when even one person turns to Christ! Imagine the joy you will share with Christ when your faithfulness to share His love and His message with others helps someone find forgiveness and eternal life.

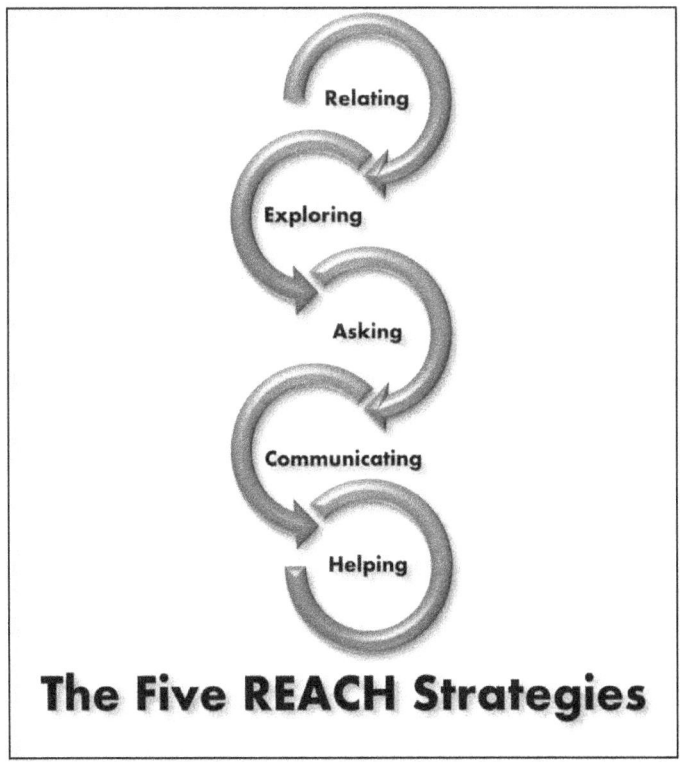

The Five REACH Strategies

Relating in Love

NATURAL EVANGELISM IS PERSONAL, BUILT ON RELATIONSHIPS.

How do you react when a perfect stranger confronts you with questions about your eternal destiny? There was a time when people shared the good news of Jesus Christ with strangers in casual public encounters, on the bus, or by going door-to-door through neighborhoods. Many churches were successful in sharing the gospel through neighborhood blitzes.

Then came the scandals. Televangelists supposedly preaching the gospel scammed

GOSPEL PRESENTATIONS

3 ABC's of Salvation
4 Spiritual Laws
5 Steps to Peace with God
6 Stops on the Romans Road

money out of sincere donors. Prominent pastors had affairs. One worldwide church organization failed to protect the children under her care – and then covered it up for years. Churches and pastors today no longer command the respect they once enjoyed. Unchurched people largely distrust the church, creating a powerful spiritual void.

The general lack of trust extends to individual believers as well. Your neighbors, coworkers, and acquaintances view many Christians as living roughly the same lives they do: hopelessness, loneliness, sex outside marriage, crushing self-inflicted debt, conflict, divorce, hatred, drunkenness, and many other unrighteous acts by the very people who are supposed to be *holy*.[3] The media proliferates this notion by highlighting both church leaders

---

[3] *1 Peter 1:14-16.*

and members who experience great moral failures.

When you try to engage a *stranger* in a conversation about their spiritual journey, they tend to dismiss you outright. From their perspective, you must be a religious nut or fanatic. Certainly there is no need to hear anything you have to say. They may be polite to you – but there is no acceptance of the words you are speaking.

> HOW THEN CAN WE REACH A DISTRUSTFUL GENERATION WITH THE ONLY MESSAGE THAT CAN TRULY CHANGE THEIR ETERNAL DESTINY? PEOPLE WILL NOT LISTEN TO, MUCH LESS BELIEVE, THE WORDS OF ANYONE THEY DO NOT TRUST, NO MATTER HOW TRUTHFUL OR WONDERFUL THE MESSAGE.

Trust cannot be declared or bestowed – it must be earned. If someone does not trust you, you are the one who must change. You must work hard to earn their trust again. Believers today will have to work very hard to build relationships with unchurched people in order to have a platform for sharing the good news of Jesus Christ.

> NATURAL EVANGELISM IS PERSONAL, BUILT ON RELATIONSHIPS.

So the R in our REACH strategies stands for *relating* – an ongoing strategy for your life is *relating in love* to people who need Jesus.

❖ The Gospel is Personal

Consider the personal nature of God. The God who created the universe was not a hands-off type who got things started and then stepped back to see how it would all turn out. He was actively involved in the creation. His Spirit was *"hovering over the surface of [the Earth]."* (Genesis 1:2, HCSB) God created light and named it *day*. He also created darkness and named it *night*. When He created the first human, the Bible reveals that God *"breathed into his nostrils the breath of life, and the man became a living being."* (Genesis 2:7, NIV) These intensely personal acts show us that He is indeed a personal God.

> THEN THE LORD GOD FORMED A MAN FROM THE DUST OF THE GROUND AND BREATHED INTO HIS NOSTRILS THE BREATH OF LIFE, AND THE MAN BECAME A LIVING BEING.
> (GEN. 2:7, NIV)

The good news of Jesus Christ is personal so it is only natural that it be shared through personal relationships. *"OK,"* you may say, *"but where do I start in building personal relationships?"*

A religious leader asked Jesus essentially the same question. He had challenged Jesus for answers about eternal life (Luke 10:25-29). Jesus wisely had a dialogue with him to understand his view of Scripture, including:

> LOVE YOUR NEIGHBOR AS YOURSELF.
> (MAT. 19:19, NIV)

The response of the religious leader is one that you and I should consider carefully in the context of forming personal relationships: *Who is my neighbor?*

❖ Leverage Your Life Zones

In the late 19th century, C. Hart Merriam is credited with popularizing the concept of *life zones.* A life zone is a categorization of an area where similar plant and animal life can be found.[4] You can borrow this concept to apply to the spheres of influence in your own life. You need to begin developing relationships with the people you meet in your personal *life zones.*

Think about the everyday aspects of your life where you share similar interests and needs with others:

- Where you *live*
- Where you *work*
- Where you *worship*
- Where you *shop*
- Where you *play*
- Where you *serve*

---

[4] NAU.edu. *Biotic Communities of the Colorado Plateau.* Retrieved 8/23/2014 at http://cpluhna.nau.edu/Biota/merriam.htm.

Each of these life zones presents an opportunity for you to build relationships with people who need Jesus. For instance, I am an avid tennis player. It is great game that people of all skill levels can play on their own or in a league format. My father has been blessed to still be playing tennis in his eighties. As I play in various men's tennis leagues, I get to meet many new people along the way. Over the years I get to play the same people a number of times. This affords me the privilege of making friends and building a relationship with men with whom I have a common interest. Building relationships with my *tennis buddies* is just a natural part of what I do. As our relationships progress, I have the opportunity to explore their spiritual journey and relate to them my own journey with Jesus.

One of the advantages of building relationships on the tennis court is that a singles match lasts anywhere from 2 - 2½ hours. This provides plenty of time for conversation between games.

A memorable moment came when I played a very competitive match with a young man I had gotten to know over the course of several seasons. Our relationship had developed to the point that we were discussing spiritual matters and I shared the gospel with him. He actually prayed to receive Christ right on the tennis court. Then he proceeded to beat me in the final set and won the match. I lost the match but he gained eternal life. I actually felt pretty good after losing that match!

Here is a great example of how building a relationship within a natural activity in your life helps you develop prospects for the kingdom and gives you opportunities to share the gospel. Sometimes you are supremely blessed to witness the birth of a new believer.

YOU NEVER KNOW WHO NEEDS HELP AND WHO NEEDS A FRIEND.

Be alert to the people you encounter in each of your life

zones. You may see an opportunity to start a new friendship – and you never know who needs help and who needs a friend.

One of my other tennis buddies and I had been friends for some time. Our relationship had developed to the point that we talked about anything and everything. I felt the need to ask about his spiritual journey. We talked about his upbringing in a marginally religious family. After asking what he understood it would take for him to get to Heaven, I asked if I could share what the Bible has to say about this important topic. He was curious but in a lot of pain after the tennis match. So I gave him a tract that explained the gospel of grace and told him we could talk more about it later.

As he was leaving, he specifically thanked me for sharing the gospel tract with him. He then proceeded to tell me that his mother had passed away the prior week and Heaven had been on his mind lately. Though he did not pray to receive Christ at that moment, the Holy Spirit had obviously been working on him long before our conversation. It is no wonder the Holy Spirit prompted me at that particular point in time to inquire about his spiritual journey.

❖ Practice Unconditional Love

Keep in mind that you are not building relationships with the sole purpose of winning a convert. Some of the people you befriend may even turn out to be Christians already. The point is to build relationships in order to pass on the love of Christ that was shown to you and that He desires to be shown to every person on the planet. Whether someone ever receives the LORD Jesus or not, this must not be a condition of your love toward that person. In the context of this unconditional love, you eventually earn the right to explore their spiritual journey – and help them along the path to finding the LORD Jesus.

Relating to people with unconditional love can be a monumental endeavor. Some people may strike you as undeserving of your love. Such people are sometimes referred to as *heavenly sandpaper.* Yet the Bible teaches that every person is made in the image of God[5] and is deserving of basic respect and human decency.

Remember what Jesus said about unconditional love? In the Sermon on the Mount, He taught that you should show love to everyone, even your enemies:

43 "You have heard that it was said, 'Love your neighbor and hate your enemy.' 44 But I tell you, love your enemies and pray for those who persecute you, 45 that you may be children of your Father in heaven. He causes his sun to rise on the evil and the good, and sends rain on the righteous and the unrighteous. 46 If you love those who love you, what reward will you get? Are not even the tax collectors doing that? 47 And if you greet only your own people, what are you doing more than others? Do not even pagans do that? 48 Be perfect, therefore, as your heavenly Father is perfect. (Matthew 5:43-48, NIV)

---

[5] *Genesis 1:27; 9:6; Acts 17:29; 1 Corinthians 11:7.*

At one point in my career I worked with a gentleman who was an avowed atheist. He seemed to enjoy mocking Christianity and public Christian leaders, especially when they had a moral failure. I committed to the LORD that I would show Christ-like love to him anyway. Over time we developed a good friendship. It was never easy. But disciple-making is always a long-term investment no matter who is involved.

The key here is that a relationship built on Christ-like love is a safe place for the seeker to open up about his or her spiritual journey. Your investment of time, patience, and unconditional love will inevitably lead to opportunities to

> A RELATIONSHIP BUILT ON CHRIST-LIKE LOVE IS A SAFE PLACE FOR THE SEEKER TO OPEN UP ABOUT HIS/HER SPIRITUAL JOURNEY.

explore the spiritual condition of your coworker, neighbor or friend.

❖ Use Your Unique Personality

Here is a bit of encouragement to the introverts of the world: building relationships probably seems to be an overwhelming and impossible task for you. It hardly seems fair that naturally extroverted people find it so much easier to reach out to new people.

BEING AN INTROVERT DOES NOT MEAN THAT YOU DISLIKE PEOPLE.

Remember, being an introvert does not mean that you do not like people or that you are unable to relate to people. It does mean that being around other people tends to drain you rather energize you.

You may not be able to pursue more than a few relationships at a time (or perhaps only one). But that is perfectly fine for you. God expects you to use only the gifts and abilities that He has uniquely equipped you to utilize.

Over time, you will learn to balance spending time with new people versus spending time alone where you can recharge your batteries.

Building deep relationships in the context of your normal life pursuits *(think life zones)* enables you to build *trust* with people. People will not listen to you if they do not trust you. However, if you have worked to gain their trust, and they have experienced your unconditional love, you have a natural avenue to introduce them to the LORD Jesus, whose love you have experienced so deeply.

Start local and build relationships in the life zones where you spend most of your time. This will facilitate natural opportunities for ongoing relationships. Natural evangelism is always personal, built on relationships.

Exploring the Spiritual Journey

NATURAL EVANGELISM EXPLORES THE SPIRITUAL JOURNEY OF YOUR FRIENDS.

Has there been a time in your life when you took the opportunity to share the good news of Jesus Christ with someone who needed Jesus? For many of you, the answer is *no*. Let's be honest at this point. When you hear someone speak about verbally sharing the way to get to Heaven with people who need Jesus, many *(if not most)* believers draw back in fear. Some even push back on the whole idea that the average Christian is even required to verbally share the good news. *After all* (they reason), *St. Francis of Assisi told us to "Preach the gospel. If necessary, use words." Let the goodness of my life be my witness to Jesus.*

There are a couple of problems with this line of thinking:

> *1) Your life will never be good enough to save someone.*

No offense intended but the only person whose life was good enough to save anyone was Jesus. And you are not Jesus *(neither am I)*.

> *2) St. Francis of Assisi never said anything like this quote.*

The closest any of his writings ever came to this concept was one of his rules on preaching that one's deeds should match his words. [6]

So the E in the REACH strategies stands for

---

[6] *TheGospelCoalition.org.* Factchecker: Misquoting Francis of Assisi. *July 10, 2012. Retrieved 8/29/2014 at http://thegospelcoalition.org/article/factchecker-misquoting-francis-of-assisi.*

exploring – at the right time you must *explore the spiritual condition* of your friends.

❖ The Gospel Requires Words

The Bible is pretty clear that one finds forgiveness, eternal life, and Heaven through a personal relationship with Jesus. The personal relationship is not even possible unless a person hears the word of God. No one is able to figure out how to get to Heaven on their own. Nature provides a general revelation of God[7] but not the plan of salvation. Rather, the Bible says:

> *"The word is near you; it is in your mouth and in your heart," that is, the <u>message concerning faith that we proclaim</u> (Rom. 10:8, NIV, emphasis mine)*

---

[7] *Psalm 19:1-4; Romans 1:18-20.*

Natural Evangelism

NATURE PROVIDES A GENERAL REVELATION OF GOD BUT NOT THE PLAN OF SALVATION.

The Apostle Paul and his missionary companions had to *proclaim* the good news to people in words not just deeds. In fact, the Bible goes on to say:

How, then, can they call on the one they have not believed in? And how can they believe in the one of whom they have not <u>heard</u>? And how can they hear without someone <u>preaching</u> to them? (Romans 10:14, NIV, emphasis mine)

Sharing a good, Christian life to win your neighbor to Christ is a noble but misguided strategy. People need the word of God to understand the way to salvation. Not everyone is called to preach but all are called to proclaim. Share your life but also share the good news.

❖ Everyone is on a Spiritual Journey

The people that you meet in your life zones are all on a journey through life. While the body grows old and eventually succumbs to the grave, your soul – the real you on the inside - is eternal. Moreover, the Bible tells us that God has placed eternity in our hearts[8] meaning all people have a basic drive to find something beyond the physical world in which we live. He has proactively given the revelation of Himself through creation,[9] conscience,[10] and Christ.[11]

God's supreme desire is for every person to enter into a relationship with Him:

3 This is good, and pleases God our Savior, 4 who wants all people to be saved and to come to a knowledge of the truth. 5 For there is one God

---

[8] *Ecclesiastes 3:11.*
[9] *Psalm 19:1-4; Romans 1:18-20.*
[10] *Romans 2:15.*
[11] *John 1:1,14,17-18.*

Natural Evangelism

and one mediator between God and mankind, the man Christ Jesus, 6 who gave himself as a ransom for all people. (1 Tim. 2:3-6, NIV)

God breathes life into every human being.[12] This means you are the pinnacle of His creation.[13] I know there are days you look in the mirror and have a hard time believing you are the *pinnacle* of anything but that is how God sees you because He created you. So it makes perfect sense when we read that God desires that everyone be saved.[14] He does not

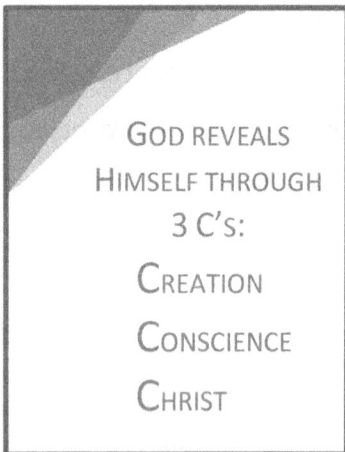

GOD REVEALS HIMSELF THROUGH 3 C'S:
CREATION
CONSCIENCE
CHRIST

---

[12] *Isaiah 42:5; John 6:63; Acts 17:25; 1 Timothy 6:13.*
[13] *After each major creation event, God pronounced that it was good. But at the end of the creation week He made the first man and woman and pronounced His creation "very good." (Gen. 1:31, NIV)*
[14] *John 3:16; 1 Timothy 2:4.*

force anyone to accept His offer so, consequentially, not everyone will be saved. Nevertheless, our journey through life is primarily a spiritual quest to get to know our Creator God.

So everyone is on a spiritual journey, even those who don't realize it. How does God connect with the unbeliever's heart on this journey? He applies a one-two punch to break through any spiritual barriers that hinder the unbeliever from entering into a relationship with Himself: the Holy Spirit and you.

1. The Holy Spirit has a ministry to bring conviction to everyone.

7 But very truly I tell you, it is for your good that I am going away. Unless I go away, the Advocate will not come to you; but if I go, I will send him to you. 8 When he comes, he will prove the world to be in the wrong about sin and righteousness and judgment:9 about sin, because people do not believe in me; 10 about righteousness, because I am going to the Father, where you can see me no longer; 11 and about judgment, because the prince of this world now stands condemned. 12 "I have much more to say to you, more than you can now bear. 13 But when he, the Spirit of truth, comes, he will guide you into all the truth. (John 16:7-13, NIV)

The Holy Spirit is at work in every person on the planet to convince them of God's truth. No matter whom you encounter, you can be sure the Holy Spirit has gone before you to bring that person under conviction. Some are ignoring His work while others are slowly coming around. Until you explore their spiritual condition, you may never know where they are in their spiritual journey.

2. You have a ministry to bring a testimony to others about Jesus.

Through faith in the LORD Jesus, you have been called and equipped to be His witness:

8 But you will receive power when the Holy Spirit comes on you; and <u>you will be my witnesses</u> in Jerusalem, and in all Judea and Samaria, and to the ends of the earth." (Acts 1:8, NIV)

45 Then he opened their minds so they could understand the Scriptures. 46 He told them, "This is what is written: The Messiah will suffer and rise from the dead on the third day, 47 and repentance for the forgiveness of sins will be preached in his name to all nations, beginning at Jerusalem. 48 <u>You are witnesses</u> of these things. (Luke 24:45-48, NIV)

As you work the REACH strategies, you will have people with whom you have been building credibility (HELPING) and a deeper relationship (RELATING), communicating in a positive manner (COMMUNICATING) and inviting them to be a part of your life, community service, and your church (ASKING). It is important to continue to pray for those who are without Christ so that you can be:

- Empowered to witness to them
- Enlightened to the appropriate time

The LORD will guide you and prompt you when to EXPLORE their spiritual condition.

❖ Starting the Conversation

Be filled with the Spirit. (Eph. 5:18, NIV)

You can either be self-absorbed or you can be a witness for Jesus. If you are led by the Holy Spirit, you will be alert to what is going on in the lives of people around you. Perhaps this is an area of growth for you in your own spiritual journey?

Whenever you build a relationship with someone, you will naturally want to hear their story. They also want to hear your story. Because you are a Christian, at some point, they may want to know the how and why of becoming a Christian.

> WHEN YOU BUILD A RELATIONSHIP WITH SOMEONE, YOU NATURALLY WANT TO HEAR THEIR STORY. THEY ALSO WANT TO HEAR YOUR STORY.

What are some ways to open up that conversation? While many provocative questions have been posed, the most common-sense approach is to find a topic that easily relates to matters of faith.

Current movies or TV shows provide an opportunity to begin a conversation about the spiritual journey. There have been many spiritually themed movies such as *Noah*, *Heaven*, *Son of God*, and *God's Not Dead* just in the past year. But it does not necessarily have to be a show with a Christian or spiritual theme. Just stay alert to opportunities to use a topic from the show as a springboard to a conversation about spiritual matters.

I was watching an old western TV show with my brother-in-law that had a self-proclaimed "faith healer" who came to town and really stirred things up. That provided an opportunity to ask what he thought about faith healers and to consider what true faith might be. This led to a conversation about the gospel and he prayed to receive Christ. It was such a beautiful moment to see this big man with tears of joy streaming down his cheeks as he understood God's forgiveness of his sins.

Current events offer many opportunities to turn the conversation to one's spiritual journey. Just consider how many *"man's inhumanity to man"* stories are in the news every day. You can ask an honest *"Does God really care?"* question.

As I write this chapter, one of the heartbreaking events in our area is a father who left his toddler in the car on a very hot summer day in the South. The young boy died and the father is on trial for murder. As you talk about such newsworthy events, be sure to steer the conversation toward God's redemptive love in a world that often seems incomprehensibly cruel.

Church can be a natural topic, even an anticipated one. As I relate to someone, the topic of church is a perfectly natural thing for me to discuss. If we are getting to know each other, church is something important to me. Mentioning something significant the church is doing for the community is a great way to start a conversation about the spiritual journey. Churches that are actually helping people in the community usually get the attention of unchurched people.

You can often gauge their readiness by how they react to the mention of *church* - not always, but most of the time. The follow-up question is only natural:

Natural Evangelism

Are you active in a church somewhere?

This is where you will see people squirm a bit – since *"active"* implies commitment. Unchurched people may go with their family to church at Christmas and Easter (C&E) but that is the limit of their religious duty. Nevertheless if you ask with sincerity and compassion, you can help them to realize your *"ask"* is within the context of a caring relationship.

> MAKE SURE YOUR *"ASK"* IS AFTER YOU HAVE ALREADY SHOWN HOW MUCH YOU CARE.

When their response is *"No"* or some sort of lukewarm response (only C&E visits to church), you now have the opportunity to dig deeper in your relationship by sincerely asking: *Why is that?*

❖ Understanding their condition

Listen to their story and try to understand how and why they are where they are. Be empathetic - you are not their judge. But keep in mind that while God meets us where we are, He loves us too much to leave us there. So in the course of this conversation, ask the next diagnostic question:

WHAT DO YOU UNDERSTAND IT WILL TAKE FOR YOU TO GET TO HEAVEN?

You are simply asking their opinion to gain an understanding of where they are on their spiritual journey. Most people have some concept of heaven and some hope, however small, of going there someday. The point of this question is to get them thinking about their relationship with God in time and for eternity.

Natural Evangelism

You will encounter a few common responses to this question:

- *I have to be good (or do good) ...*
- *I don't really know ...*
- *Believe in Jesus!*

The funniest response I ever heard was when an older lady told me, *"Well, I guess I have to die first!"* That was new – and pretty funny – so we both had a good laugh about it.

Whether someone gives you some sort of *"believe in Jesus"* answer or not, it is natural and necessary to confirm with them what the Bible actually says about salvation. There are many distorted views of Heaven, Jesus, and salvation that people receive. Only the word of God can point us to the actual truth that leads people to forgiveness and eternal life.

❖ Sharing the good news

Having reached a point in your relationship where you have discovered the other person's understanding of how one can reach Heaven someday, it is now time to direct them to the only way to Heaven.[15] To share the plan of salvation with your friends, simply ask them:

> MAY I SHARE WITH YOU WHAT I READ IN THE BIBLE ABOUT GETTING TO HEAVEN?

At this point in your relationship, they will most likely say "Yes!" If not, you can pray for them and move on to other subjects. But if they are willing to hear, there are many ways to share the good news. Just find one that is the most natural to you.

---

[15] *Jesus made it clear that He is the only way to Heaven (John 14:6).*

Memorizing an Outline

For one to be a messenger, one must have a message. If you want to be able to carry the good news around with you wherever you go, then memorizing an outline is an obvious choice. It is like sharing a recipe with someone. But memorizing is not for everyone. If you have tried to memorize outlines but just cannot find the words when you have the opportunity to share, then perhaps you can try one of the other methods covered later in this chapter.

There are many outlines to choose from:

- *3 ABC's of salvation*
- *4 spiritual laws*
- *5 steps to peace with God*
- *6 stops on the Romans road*

- *7 to heaven[16]*

The particular outline you use is not important. Just keep it brief[17] and clearly communicate the main points of the gospel including:

- God is holy and man is sinful.
- Jesus is the way to fix it – through the cross and His resurrection.
- A person must turn from sin (self-willed life) and believe the good news about the LORD Jesus.

The way I generally take someone through the good news is using the acrostic GRACE (see Appendix A for a detailed presentation of the GRACE outline). God's grace is an attractive way to present the path to salvation for the

---

[16] *I have not actually seen this one yet but I am sure there must be a gospel presentation in 7 parts somewhere.*
[17] *In today's digital age, people tend to have short attention spans. A long, drawn-out presentation – no matter how biblically accurate – will cause the hearer to zone out of perhaps the most important conversation they will ever have.*

unchurched person today since many see God (and the Bible) as very judgmental.

Drawing a Picture

If you have trouble memorizing and/or communicating an entire outline, the picture method may be more your style. You only need to remember one Scripture verse. This method is called *One-Verse Evangelism*, developed by Randy Raysbrook (Navigators). Use Romans 6:23 to walk someone word by word through the good news.

> FOR THE WAGES OF SIN IS DEATH, BUT THE GIFT OF GOD IS ETERNAL LIFE IN CHRIST JESUS OUR LORD. (ROMANS 6:23, NIV)

You start by writing the verse on a napkin or piece of paper. Next you circle the main words (*wages, sin, death, gift, God, eternal life, Jesus*

Christ, Lord) one at a time and begin to draw elements of a simple picture. As the picture unfolds, you lead the person through an understanding of the main points of the good news.

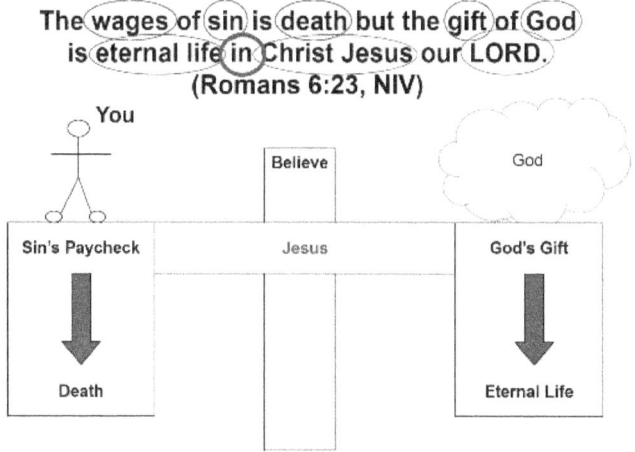

The One-Verse Evangelism approach is described in detail on the website Navigators.org. Simply enter "One-Verse Evangelism" into the search box and you will find several pages that will help you learn this simple but fun approach.

Sharing a Booklet

For anyone who feels uncomfortable without having something in writing to use in sharing the good news, sharing a booklet may be the answer for you. There are many great booklets (also called tracts) that present the main points of the good news. You can find booklets tailored to specific audiences or of a more general nature. I have relied upon the American Tract Society[18] for purchasing good news booklets and found their resources to be biblical and conservative.

Once you are at a point of sharing the good news, you can introduce your friend to a booklet. It would be best to go over the contents with them, step-by-step. My favorite booklet is Billy Graham's *Steps to Peace With God*. Most

---

[18] *The American Tract Society is now publishing their booklets through Crossway. You can find them at: http://www.crossway.org/group/ats.*

people will know who Billy Graham is and have some level of respect for him as a man of integrity and consistency. You can simply ask, *"Have you ever heard of Billy Graham? He wrote this little booklet that I think you will find helpful."* Then take them page-by-page through the booklet.

If the occasion does not provide time to go through the good news personally, leave the booklet with them. Specifically ask them to read it later and be sure to follow-up. With the booklet approach, you do not need to commit anything to memory. Everything that needs to be said is on the pages of the booklet.

Whether it is a recipe, picture, or booklet, find a method for sharing the good news that works for you so you can *"Always be prepared to give*

an answer to everyone who asks you to give the reason for the hope that you have. But do this with gentleness and respect." (1 Peter 3:15, NIV)

Natural evangelism explores the spiritual journey of your friends and neighbors.

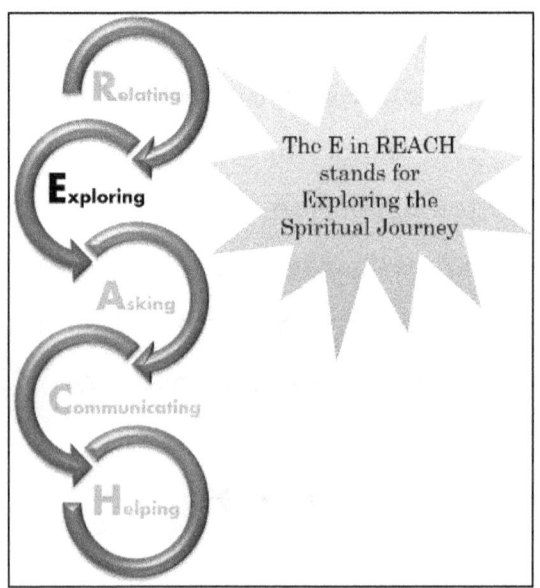

Asking People to the Party

NATURAL EVANGELISM PROVIDES UNIVERSAL INVITATIONS

Natural evangelism examines the key relationships you develop each day to look for opportunities to point people to Jesus. Asking people to join you in meaningful activities is a great way to pique the interest of unchurched people and expose them to the love and message of Christ.

Jesus made it clear that there will be great, big parties in Heaven. You do not have to worry about boring afternoons sitting on a cloud strumming a harp. He said, *"I tell you that in the same way there will be more rejoicing in heaven over one sinner who repents than over ninety-nine righteous persons who do not need to repent." (Luke 15:7, NIV).* If this is the case for a single person who enters into a relationship with God, imagine what Heaven will be like on the day every believer is gathered together with the LORD!

The A in the REACH strategies stands for *asking* – making personal invitations to all the people you encounter in your life zones. Ask people to join you for special events in your life, community service, and appropriate church activities & events.

❖ Come and See

The gospel accounts of Jesus' life and the subsequent books in the New Testament all provide many great examples of believers asking people to join them – to *"come and see:"*

45 Philip found Nathanael and told him, "We have found the one Moses wrote about in the Law, and about whom the prophets also wrote—Jesus of Nazareth, the son of Joseph." 46 "Nazareth! Can anything good come from there?" Nathanael asked. "Come and see," said Philip. (John 1:45-46, NIV)

28 Then, leaving her water jar, the woman went back to the town and said to the people, 29 "Come, see a man who told me everything I ever did. Could this be the Messiah?" (John 4:28-29, NIV)

Sometimes it really is as simple as asking people to join you at your church. If someone you meet and get to know over time receives your sincere invitation to go with you to church,

Natural Evangelism

he/she might just say, *"Yes!"* If you ask a stranger, you will probably not get as many takers. The *relationships* you build (the R in the REACH strategies) are crucial to the *Asking* strategy.

Special events at your church, especially the Christmas and Easter seasons, provide a natural vehicle to use in the asking process. People tend to be less reluctant to try a church when it is a special event and many other people may be visiting as well. These two seasons also induce much anxiety and guilt giving many people pause to consider going to church. Regardless of the motivation, it is good that people at least try the church experience where they can be

> SOMETIMES IT REALLY IS AS SIMPLE AS ASKING PEOPLE TO JOIN YOU FOR CHURCH OR SPECIAL EVENTS.

exposed to the love of God's people and the message of Christ.

Try not to be discouraged if the person says "no thanks" or does not come with you even though they said they would. Continue loving them, praying for them, and inviting them. One day they may surprise you.

❖ Small Groups Have a Big Impact

The single most important way to get unchurched people engaged at church is to connect them with an appropriate small group. Appropriate groups are those where the unchurched person has some affinity – age, marital status, children/no children, hobbies, new believers, seekers. The possibilities for different types of affinity groups are endless. Part of your church's small group strategy should be to target natural affinity groups and use those to attract people. General groups with no particular affinity target tend to stagnate and dwindle over time. Small groups need focus and purpose to be effective - just as individuals do.

You should be familiar with the different types of small groups available at your church so you can ask your friend or neighbor to try a group that will be naturally attractive to them. If it is a group you also attend, so much the better.

> SMALL GROUPS NEED FOCUS AND PURPOSE TO BE EFFECTIVE.

In fact, even if you invite your friend to a group that is right for them but not for you, it is a good idea to go with them to that group to ensure they are as comfortable as possible. Once they get connected to people in their group, you have the option of going back to your own small group.

Small groups that have specific focus and purpose can be *sticky* if the group handles prospects carefully. A person who visits a group is a prospect. The small group then has the responsibility to shepherd that prospect much as they would for the current members of the group. This shows that every person matters and helps the prospect to become assimilated into the group.

When you ask your friend or neighbor to join you in a small group, be sure to reach out to the leadership of that group. Let them know as much information about the prospect as you can. Also hold them accountable for reaching out and following up with the prospect. It is hard enough for an unchurched person to be in a church setting. The people in the small group must work diligently to engage and integrate the prospect with the members of the group.

Once the prospect is sufficiently plugged-in to the group through new friends and regular attendance, you can feel comfortable rejoining your own group. A properly functioning small group will care equally well for its members and prospects.

By helping your friend/neighbor get connected with a small group (and, by definition, exposed to the love and message of Christ), you have put your friend/neighbor on the path toward Heaven – all with a simple but sincere invitation!

❖ A Community Connection

Another avenue for asking people to the party is to invite your friends and neighbors to join you in serving your community. As you practice the H in the REACH strategies *(Helping in Tangible Ways)*, ask people you know to join you. When your friends and neighbors join you on your service project, it accomplishes several important goals:

- *You demonstrate the difference that Jesus has made in your own life (compelling you to help others).*

- *You show the difference that Jesus makes in a community through His people (the Church).*

- *You expose your friend/neighbor to other believers who can connect with them as well.*

Remember, you are not a lone ranger Christian. It takes many people loving, praying, and sharing with someone to bring them to the major life decision of believing the gospel of Jesus Christ.

What types of service projects are appropriate to help your friend or neighbor in their spiritual journey? There really is no limit to the types of projects you can undertake. See the chapter on

Helping in Tangible Ways for some ideas on how you can get involved. As long as you are making a tangible difference in your community, you will be involving your friend/neighbor in the redemptive work of Christ.

Be sure to discuss with your friend/neighbor why you are helping out in your community. You will want to help them see that the love of Christ **for** you is the basis of the love of Christ demonstrated **through** you. His grace is love that is given freely though undeserved. Your service to others should reflect this same sacrificial commitment to other people.

It is a grand thing to see people make connections with people in church, small groups, and even in service projects. Become an agent in your life zones – an agent of the universal invitation of Jesus: *"Whoever hears my word and believes him who sent me has eternal life and will not be judged but has crossed over from death to life."* (John 5:24, NIV)

Natural evangelism provides universal invitations to people who need Jesus.

Communicating the Positive

NATURAL EVANGELISM ADVANCES
WITH POSITIVE, HOPE-FILLED WORDS.

With an eternity in Heaven as the certain hope for every believer in Jesus Christ,[19] the present reality is that *"our citizenship is in heaven."* (Phil. 3:20, NIV) Christians should be the most upbeat, joyous, positive creatures in the world. Words of hope should roll off our tongues like the spring rains. If only this were true! Anyone who has been to a contentious church business meeting *(especially around budget time)* knows the hurtful words that pour forth from professing Christians. We can all remember

---

[19] *Romans 5:1-2; Ephesians 1:18; Titus 3:7; 1 Peter 1:3-5.*

multiple times when church people acted in decidedly unchristian ways.

❖ Your Worldview Matters

Seeing a Christian live for years with a sour disposition and a negative outlook on life makes you wonder: *do such Christians have the right worldview?* Your worldview is the set of principles and truths that shape how you perceive and interact with the world in which you live. If you have no faith in God, for instance, you probably have no hope beyond the grave. Your worldview is that life is pretty meaningless. Morality becomes amorality and life choices really do not matter in the end so anything goes in the present. Many who live in generational poverty and dangerous neighborhoods develop a gripping despair because no one seems to care. As a result, their life choices often turn to destructive, self-gratifying behaviors.

❖ Your Future is Bright

On the other hand, if you have faith in the LORD Jesus who paid for all sins on the cross and conquered the grave through the His resurrection, you have the certainty that the grave will not hold your soul. He has promised Heaven as the future home of all who believe in Him. Life is no longer a meaningless journey that ends in nothingness. Jesus gives us hope for the future and purpose for the present – truly a life worth living.[20] You shape all of your morality, life

> IS IT EVER REASONABLE FOR A CHRISTIAN TO LIVE WITHOUT HOPE?

---

[20] *John 10:10.*

choices, and inner peace around the truth of what Jesus Christ has already accomplished on your behalf.

So with a worldview based on the unchangeable gift of salvation through Jesus Christ and the promise of Heaven from a God who cannot lie, you live in the present world full of hope. You can have passion in life because of the passion of Christ. This is God's marvelous gift to all who believe.

❖ Your Speech Should Be Bright

In the REACH strategies, the R stands for relating to people in love. How will your worldview enhance your ability to form relationships? The Bible teaches us that the words you speak flow from deep within your heart.[21] The heart of a Christian should be overflowing with grace[22] and the marvelous truth about our Savior who gives us the certain hope of Heaven.

For the mouth speaks from the overflow of the heart. (Matthew 12:34, HCSB)

Do you speak with your neighbor out of an abundance of grace and hope? What about that customer service representative with the difficult accent? How about the child who was in your way when you were in a hurry? While Christians *should* be full of grace and hope, we often succumb to manners of speech and not so choice words that repel people rather than redeem them.

A WORD FITLY SPOKEN IS LIKE APPLES OF GOLD IN SETTINGS OF SILVER. (PROV. 25:11, NIV)

---

[21] *Matthew 15:18; Mark 7:21; Luke 6:45.*
[22] *Romans 5:17; 2 Corinthians 9:8; 1 Timothy 1:14.*

Natural Evangelism

Consider with brutal honesty what your manner of speech is toward people. Grace-filled speech will take you farther and deeper in your relationships than coarse, uncaring words.

THINK ABOUT WHAT YOU SAY AND HOW YOU SAY IT BEFORE YOU SAY IT.

People today deal with plenty of uncaring, foul-mouthed people. Sadly many become like the very people they encounter. It is crucial that every Christian become the positive, hope-filled light the world so desperately needs.

You do not have to share the gospel with every person you encounter to shine the light of Jesus in their direction. Speak words out of the overflow of God's unmerited favor directed toward you because of the sacrifice of the LORD Jesus. Let the hope of Heaven be a bright beacon that guides your tongue along positive paths. In this way, each person you encounter will be left with a measure of hope and, perhaps, wonder about his/her future direction.

You can try to build relationships with a scowl or a smile, a careless word or a care-filled word – which path leads to a relationship where you can help someone along in their spiritual journey toward Christ?

❖ Be Positive but Real

Have you ever met a Christian with such a positive outlook on life that you wonder if they live on the same planet as you?

I used to encounter a friend at work whose greeting to me was always, "Life is good!" His eyebrow would raise and a twinkle would appear in his eyes as if to say, "And how about you?" I was very happy for him but, at the time, life was not good for me at all. I decided not to burst his bubble by moaning about all the difficulties I faced so I just said, "Great!" and moved on.

Natural Evangelism

Consider this situation: Your house burns down, you lose your job, and, to top it all off, your dog runs away! Try to think of some positive, grace-filled words to say to your neighbor as he watches the plumes of smoke rise from what used to be your living room.

A positive outlook based on grace and hope in the LORD Jesus does not mean you ignore the realities of life. We live in a sin-cursed world. Jesus told us very plainly that we would experience trouble in this world. But He also said, *"I have overcome the world"* (John 16:33, NIV) and *"surely I am with you always, to the very end..."* (Matthew 28:20, NIV)

> A POSITIVE OUTLOOK BASED ON GRACE AND HOPE DOES NOT MEAN YOU IGNORE THE REALITIES OF LIFE.

Sometimes a Christian will cry in tragedy. Other times a Christian will grow angry and bitter over unfair circumstances. Even in such times, Jesus, the One who overcame the world, is with you. You have that going for you no matter how bad things may be. And you are forgiven in Christ with the hope of Heaven ahead. You have this firm foundation on which to stand, even when the ground is literally quaking beneath you.

So I am not suggesting you say only positive things that put you out of touch with the reality in which you and your neighbor live. What I am pointing out is that you must use your worldview to shape your thinking and the words that you speak, especially in difficult times. You will gain far more

> YOUR PRESENT REALITY IS ALWAYS GROUNDED IN YOUR CERTAIN FUTURE WITH CHRIST.

relational traction with your neighbors and friends by acknowledging the reality of your present circumstances in the context of your faith in God's wisdom, power, and presence in your life. Your present reality is always grounded in your future reality – the certainty of Heaven because of the work of Christ on your behalf.

❖ Connect the Dots of Faith

The words you speak with people in your life zones should work to connect their present reality with the possible future they can have with Christ. You start by pointing out how God is working:

- In your own life to mold you into a more loving, caring person
- In your church to make a difference in the lives of people in the local community

When the unchurched, unsaved person sees a church that actually helps people in tangible ways, it serves as a spiritual wake-up call. Help and hope work to overcome the negative attitudes toward church. A few bad apples do not negate the work of millions of faithful church leaders and impactful churches across the world. Pointing out specific activity with local impact provides indisputable facts to overcome the usual media narrative.

From the mouth of the righteous comes the fruit of wisdom. (Proverbs 10:31, NIV)

Through positive, hope-filled words, you can help your neighbor to see the grace and power of God at work in tangible ways:

- Perhaps your church works with a charitable organization to feed hungry people in your community. Let your neighbor know about such efforts as it shows that you and your church really care about people.

- Many churches provide English schools and citizenship classes as a community outreach. This shows your neighbor that church is not an exclusive club for *church* people – everyone is invited to be a part of God's kingdom.

- Churches conduct classes and conferences open to the community on building strong marriages, dealing with issues faced by blended families, single parenting, or healthy living. Let your neighbors know about these offerings – even if they do not take advantage of them they will begin to gain respect for your church.

Be sure to help your neighbor understand the why behind you and your church's efforts to help people. Your worldview shapes your world behavior. It is not about being good in order to impress God. It is about the certainty of Heaven that drives you to reach out to people in the real world.

❖ ❖ ❖

With an accurate understanding of the Christian worldview, your words will trend positive and be filled with hope. Practice communicating with people using this strategy. You may have some rough edges to your speech right now but every Christian can learn to speak in ways that promote trust and respect.

THE LIPS OF THE RIGHTEOUS KNOW WHAT FINDS FAVOR. (PROVERBS 10:32, NIV)

Natural evangelism advances God's kingdom with positive, hope-filled words.

Natural Evangelism

Helping in Tangible Ways

NATURAL EVANGELISM IS FUELLED BY
CREDIBILITY IN YOUR COMMUNITY.

It was nearly Christmas one year and a young family was having some serious financial difficulties. The father had lost his job and one of the children had some acute health problems – with some rather acute bills. The mother confided in a coworker about the challenges her family faced this year in what was supposed to be the season of Christmas cheer.

Fortunately the coworker was a Christian who took the challenges of this young family to heart. She organized a secret campaign to buy Christmas presents for the children and gift cards for gas and groceries to give the parents. She enlisted the help of her church. A Christmas miracle package was given to the mother anonymously a few days before Christmas. The children woke up to a bright morning of gifts as their parents found hope in the generosity of strangers.

The mother and her coworker became good friends over time. She spoke positively about the work her church was doing in the community for struggling families. The mother wondered if her church might have been the one to help out at Christmas time. Her curiosity and gratitude led her family to visit that church and become an active part of the caring congregation.

Helping people in tangible ways may not seem, at first, like an effective evangelism strategy. To be sure, this has nothing to do with sharing the gospel or leading someone in the sinner's prayer. As part of the REACH strategies, helping people in your life zones serves to build credibility – the quality of being believable and trustworthy.

> WHAT VALUE DO YOU PLACE ON BEING BELIEVABLE AND TRUSTWORTHY?

If it is your desire to be a more effective witness, what value would you place on being known as someone who is both *believable* and *trustworthy*?

❖ Jesus Modelled Community Service

The model of helping people in tangible ways is rooted in the work of Jesus Christ during His earthly ministry. His mission was to seek and to save the lost by proclaiming the kingdom of God.[23] Yet we see Jesus working in His community to help and to teach about the kingdom of God:

---

[23] *Luke 19:10, Mark 1:14-15.*

> *³⁵Jesus went through all the towns and villages, teaching in their synagogues, proclaiming the good news of the kingdom and healing every disease and sickness. ³⁶When he saw the crowds, he had compassion on them, because they were harassed and helpless, like sheep without a shepherd. (Matthew 9:35-36, NIV)*

What were the needs that Jesus saw and met in His community?

- *Truth* – by teaching the word of God (v.35)

- *Relationship with God* - by preaching the good news (v.35)

- *Healing* – by dealing with every disease & sickness (v.35)

- *Comfort* – by showing compassion (v.36)

- *Help* – because He showed compassion (v.36)

- Guidance – by shepherding them (v.36)

Think about how these needs compare with your community. It is over 2,000 years later and the basic needs of people have not changed. If we want to be effective in our mission – to seek and to save the lost[24] – then we must work to meet the real needs of people in our community just like Jesus did.

In a skeptical, untrusting world, many people dismiss the claims of Christianity – unconditional love, forgiveness of sins, hope for the future even in the afterlife. Such skeptics cannot dismiss acts of sacrificial, unconditional love that result in real needs being met in their own community.

Community service that Jesus modeled worked in the first century to build credibility and

---

[24] *Luke 19:10.*

noticeability. His work got the attention of people who had long ago lost hope.

- A *Samaritan woman* at a well was shocked that Jesus talked with her about issues that mattered to her. For generations her people had been scorned and avoided by the Jews.

- He spoke at length and at night with a *religious leader* who had been observing Jesus' ministry. He spent time with the man who had many questions about issues of eternal significance.

- Jesus worked to bring healing and help to *beggars, widows, and foreigners.* Those in need who asked for His help were never turned away.

❖ Compassion Drives Outreach

Why did Jesus work so hard to find and meet the needs of people? His motivation was clear: *"He had compassion on them."* (v. 36)

It is time for you to find ways to help real people in your local community. Do you find it more *convenient* to give money to some worthy cause or church program rather than get involved yourself?

Jesus never acted based on convenience. His mission created a rather large *inconvenience* for His personal life plans (whatever they might have been). Jesus was a skilled worker and could have provided a good living for Himself and a family. Instead, He followed the will of God the Father – using His adult years to teach people and mentor a group of disciples who would carry His message to the ends of the Earth. It turned out to be a dangerous mission given the religious climate in which He lived. Ultimately God's mission for His Son

JESUS NEVER ACTED BASED ON WHAT WAS CONVENIENT.

would lead Jesus to sacrifice His life on a cross. Though He asked the Father if there was any other way, He was determined to follow whatever path chosen for Him: *"Yet not as I will, but as you will."* (Matthew 26:39, NIV)

FAITH CAN BE DEFINED AS BELIEVING GOD AND DOING WHAT HE SAYS.

Do you believe God's word, the Bible? I hope so. How do you know you believe? Faith requires obedience to God's will. Knowing that Jesus modelled sacrificial, unconditional love in serving others in His life zones, will you demonstrate genuine faith in Him by finding real needs in your own community and work to meet those needs? Compassion is another word for love. It is the motivation Jesus had for serving us. It is your motivation to serve others.

❖ Plan Meaningful Involvement

What are some ways you can get involved in your community that will make a difference in the lives of people? It would be impossible to list everything you could do because the answer lies in the needs of people in your own life zones. Your life zones are different than mine. The basic needs of people are the same no matter where you are in the world: food, shelter, clothing, and a job. But the way those needs are manifest are unique to the community in which you live.

Think about ways you can get involved with your community.

For me, I live in a neighborhood that has an association of homeowners dedicated to the betterment of the community. I had lived in the neighborhood for many years without getting involved in their planning efforts or neighborhood work days. The LORD convicted me that I needed to get involved. So I volunteered to serve on the governing board during a critical time in the life of our neighborhood. They were happy to have anyone volunteer since it seemed a very unpleasant task to most people.

The issues were difficult but I considered it an honor to give back to my neighborhood and, hence, my neighbors. Over the next two years I became acquainted with more people in my neighborhood than I had in the previous twenty years. Working through the difficult issues the association faced enabled me to build credibility and visibility among my neighbors. I continue to build relationships with people to this day that are only possible because of my community involvement.

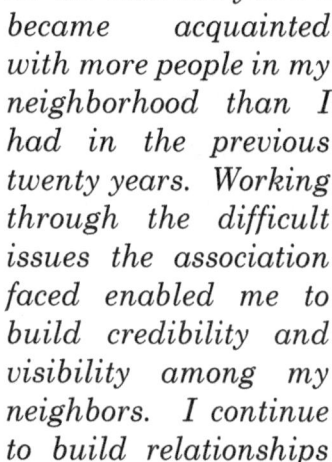

THE ANSWER TO HOW TO GET INVOLVED LIES IN THE NEEDS OF PEOPLE IN YOUR OWN LIFE ZONES.

This is just one way to get involved. Your community may have a segment of people living in poverty. If there are organizations dedicated to feeding and helping people in this situation, you could get involved that group. Or you could even start your own group to minister to the needy.

Consider the table below as it provides some key categories of personal outreach activity that you can think about in relation to your own life zones:

Outreach Category	Description
MISSIONS	*Missions is defined as crossing a cultural or geographic boundary. Some of your life zones may be in areas of town where there are large concentrations of ethnic groups different than your own. Consider ways you can get involved to help target groups with their particular needs. Examples include skills training (resume writing, interview skills, English classes) and relief work (food pantries, construction and clean-up projects).*

NATURAL EVANGELISM

Outreach Category	Description
SERVICE EVENTS	*One-day activities where you join with other believers to serve others is a great way to bring visibility to your work. You do not want visibility for the sake of being seen for your righteous deeds[25] Rather it creates interest in the community that gives you natural bridges to speak with people and begin building new relationships.*
NEIGHBORHOOD OUTREACH	*Never forget the people in your own backyard. Make specific plans to reach out to your neighbors. Be a good neighbor to your neighbors. Smile and wave – it is amazing how attitudes can change when confronted with someone who is genuinely friendly. Look for real needs – aged or worn areas that can be spruced up, older neighbors who could use a helping hand – and fill them.*

---

[25] *Matthew 6:1-4 points to the motivation behind your good deeds – to glorify God and not yourself.*

Outreach Category	Description
SPIRITUAL DISCIPLINE	*Last but not least is the matter of prayer. Pray for the people in your neighborhood and in your community. It has been said that prayer fires the winning shot. The Bible reveals that prayer comes with a guarantee that God will answer our righteous prayers.* [26] *In fact, Jesus taught a parable that we should never give up but continue to petition God for our needs.*[27] *To reach your neighborhood, pray for people by name and keep praying. Start prayer-walking your neighborhood and those around you. Through your prayers, hearts will be melted and opportunities for relationships will emerge over time.*

---

[26] *James 5:17; 1 John 5:14-15.*
[27] *The parable of the unjust judge (Luke 18:1-8) shows us that God will respond to our diligent prayers. He is just and will remember His children.*

Use these categories as a place to brainstorm your own community outreach plan. Start small, start local, and branch out as you become more confident in God's work in and through you.

❖ Credibility Drives Relationships

Credibility opens the door to greater intimacy in relationships. As you get involved with your time and talents, not just your money, you will build deep relationships with even the most skeptical people. They will simply be amazed at your lack of concern for your own well-being. The difference you make in the lives of people will plant a seed of hope that can grow into an open field for the good news of Jesus Christ.

I worked with a young man who showed a deep resentment toward Christians. Perhaps he had been raised by an irreligious family. Maybe someone who professed to be a Christian had hurt him or someone he loved. In any event, I faced his antagonism and scorn every day at work. We were on the same project team working together in a small conference room. I had nowhere else to work so I made the best of it. He would intentionally bring up provocative issues or negative stories about church leaders to taunt me. It was a very depressing environment.

Rather than become angry, I resolved to show compassion on him. I prayed for him daily and asked God for opportunities to share my faith with him. At one point he did bring up a subject that was an open door to explain the gospel. He flatly rejected it. As gently but clearly as I could, I explained to him the consequences of rejecting God's grace only left God's judgment. He dismissed this as well. So I told him I would not bring this matter up anymore but would pray for him. "Please don't!" he said. I think this is the first time anyone has ever asked me NOT to pray. Nevertheless, I continued to pray for him.

Over the next few years I continued to try and build a relationship with him. We became casual friends and talked about many things other than spiritual matters. Then our relationship changed – I became his boss. At our first private meeting to discuss expectations for his role, I told him, "I want you to know that none of our conversations in the past regarding matters of faith will in any way impact our new relationship or the work we need to get done." He looked me straight in the eye and said, "I expect nothing less." Wow, no pressure there!

After all this time of praying for him, building a relationship, and trying to establish credibility in the workplace, he was still watching me to see if I would live what I believe. I did. And he saw that he was treated in an even-handed manner just as were all the people in my group.

Building credibility takes time. It is, however, a necessary step in building relationships with the irreligious. I do have some encouraging news in this young atheist's journey:

After a couple of years later, he was with a coworker on top of Stone Mountain[28] in Georgia. She was a committed Christian as well and had many faith-oriented discussions with this man. She asked him point blank, "When you see this incredible view of creation, how can you say that

---

[28] *Stone Mountain is a large mountain made of granite, the largest exposed piece of granite in the world. It is just to the East of Atlanta, Georgia in the United States.*

there is no God?" He hesitated a bit but finally acknowledged, "Well, I think you are right – there must be a God."

It took years for this man to move from an atheistic viewpoint to at least an acknowledgement that God exists. The reason this happened is because the Spirit of God was working to bring conviction and God's people were there establishing credibility he could experience. The relationships formed would not have gone any deeper had we not had credibility in his eyes.

7 ... A man reaps what he sows ... 9 Let us not become weary in doing good, for at the proper time we will reap a harvest if we do not give up. 10 Therefore, as we have opportunity, let us do good to all people, especially to those who belong to the family of believers. (Gal. 6:7-10, NIV)

Natural Evangelism

The principle of sowing & reaping in the Bible can be applied to many areas of life but no more so than in regard to evangelism. The key is to stay the course even when you are not seeing immediate results – do not *"become weary in doing good."* (v9) Even with the Holy Spirit at work bringing conviction, people require time to change. The people in your life zones will need your patience and endurance to stay on course toward the goal: *to help them find a personal relationship with the LORD Jesus.*

> THE PRINCIPLE OF SOWING & REAPING IN THE BIBLE CAN BE APPLIED TO MANY AREAS OF LIFE BUT NO MORE SO THAN TO EVANGELISM.

Natural evangelism is fueled by your credibility in the community in which you live, work, and play.

Helping in Tangible Ways

Implementing the REACH Strategies

NATURAL EVANGELISM IS A LIFESTYLE OF SHARING THE LOVE AND MESSAGE OF CHRIST IN THE CONTEXT OF RELATIONSHIPS YOU FORM ALONG THE WAY.

How will you develop into an effective disciple-maker in your own community? The five REACH strategies will go a long way in helping you develop prospects for God's kingdom, giving you opportunities to share the good news of Jesus Christ, and enabling you to see people take that first step into a relationship with the LORD Jesus.

As I stated earlier, the five REACH strategies are not sequential in nature. REACH is not a rigid recipe to be followed starting with step 1, step 2, etc. Rather it is a set of principles by which you live your life with the intention of being the kind of disciple-maker that Jesus commanded. Ordinary people can make an extraordinary difference as these principles are practiced on a daily basis through the years.

> **REACH STRATEGIES**
>
> - R stands for Relating in Love
> - E stands for Exploring the Spiritual Journey
> - A stands for Asking People to the Party
> - C stands for Communicating the Positive
> - H stands for Helping in Tangible Ways

In most cases, the two strategies you will need to implement first are the H *(Helping in Tangible Ways)* to build credibility with people in your life zones. The second strategy is the R *(Relating in Love)* to build strong relationships from the trust you engender through your community service. These two strategies create a foundation for the other three. People are more likely to hear you when they trust you. Being a person someone can believe in is a stepping stone for that person to believe in God. You, of course, are not God and never will never rise to that level in someone's life. Yet hope is a springboard to faith. Be the kind of person that brings hope to people in your life zones.

Remember that the REACH strategies are not a short-term evangelism program but a way of life for the rest of your life. The gospel is ineffective when it only points to your own heart. You must take the gospel that changed your life and

> BEING A PERSON SOMEONE CAN BELIEVE IN IS A STEPPING STONE FOR THAT PERSON TO BELIEVE IN GOD.

share it with others so they can find the hope and peace you enjoy.

Use these REACH strategies and teach them to as many people as you can. The multiplication effect creates an opportunity to make a real difference in your community. It is my prayer that communities all over the world will begin to wake up with hope and renewed optimism that someone out there really cares.

> WHAT WE DO FOR OURSELVES DIES WITH US.
> WHAT WE DO FOR OTHERS AND THE WORLD
> REMAINS AND IS IMMORTAL.
> ~ALBERT PIKE~

You can be the one person in your community that makes the difference for time and eternity. Natural evangelism is now your new lifestyle of sharing the love and message of Christ.

IMPLEMENTING REACH STRATEGIES

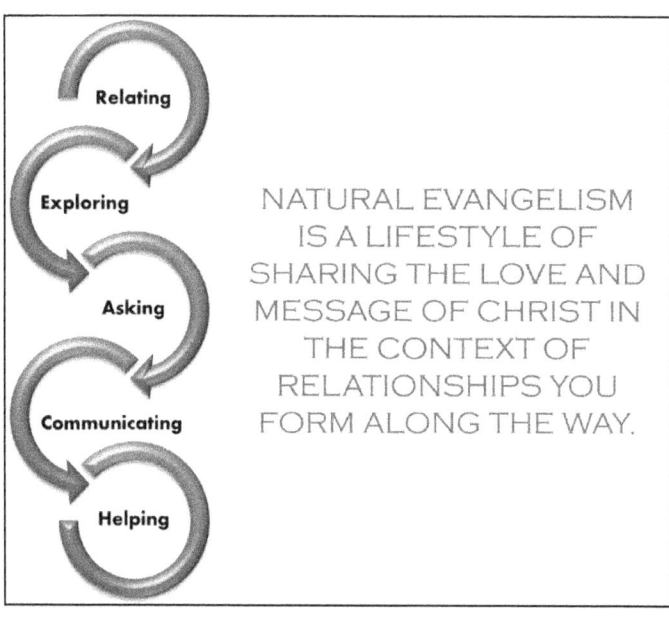

NATURAL EVANGELISM IS A LIFESTYLE OF SHARING THE LOVE AND MESSAGE OF CHRIST IN THE CONTEXT OF RELATIONSHIPS YOU FORM ALONG THE WAY.

Appendix A – The GRACE Outline

Contrary to what you often hear about God from other people, the Bible tells us that God is a God of grace. Grace is a kindness expressed to you even though you do not deserve it. Since God is holy and perfectly righteous, the only way that He could relate to anyone is by grace.

> FOR IT IS BY GRACE YOU HAVE BEEN SAVED, THROUGH FAITH—AND THIS NOT FROM YOURSELVES, IT IS THE GIFT OF GOD—NOT BY WORKS, SO THAT NO ONE CAN BOAST.
> (EPHESIANS 2:8-9, NIV)

By grace and not by works, the God who created all things allows you to enter into a relationship with Him forever. Each letter of the word GRACE illustrates a key aspect of the tremendous grace that God extends to you through His Son, Jesus Christ:

❖ The GRACE Outline

The Good News of God's	
Gracious	God loves you and everyone else (John 3:16).
Righteous	Though God is holy and you are not, He is still willing to give you eternal life (Romans 6:23).
Acceptance	Jesus makes you acceptable to God by dying for ALL your sins (1 Peter 3:18).
Certainty	Jesus rose from the dead so you can be sure you are forgiven (Romans 4:25).
Eternal Life	Eternal life is a forever relationship with God that starts the moment you choose to believe (John 5:24).

G stands for Gracious

Grace point:
God loves you and everyone else.

For God so loved the world that He gave His One and Only Son [Jesus], that whoever believes in Him shall not perish but have eternal life. (John 3:16, NIV)

Is there someone you know that is a really, really, good person? Do you think God loves that person more than you? The reality of God's grace is that He cannot love you any less than the best person you know. He is your Creator and loves you because He gave you life. God is gracious in loving people even though their attitudes and actions sometimes fall short of His righteousness. This reflects His grace extended to you...

R stands for Righteous

Grace point: Though God is righteous and you are not, He is still willing to give you eternal life.

For the wages of sin is death, but the gift of God is eternal life in Christ Jesus our Lord. (Romans 6:23, NIV)

Could God be truly loving without being righteous as well? Love is founded on righteousness. So God defines the boundaries for our behavior (thoughts, words, deeds) as righteousness. Every human being falls short – the Bible calls this sin. Nevertheless, God is willing to give you eternal life as a reflection of His grace…

A stands for Acceptance

Grace point: Jesus makes you acceptable to God by dying for ALL your sins!

For Christ died for sins once for all, the righteous for the unrighteous, to bring you to God. (1 Peter 3:18, NIV)

Can God accept you, knowing all that you have said and done in your life? God made the greatest sacrifice for you to make you acceptable. God became a man, Jesus, and lived the perfect life that you and I can never live. Then He offered His perfect life for you on a cross. His sacrifice for your sins brings forgiveness within your grasp. Grace upon grace is offered to you...

C stands for Certainty

Grace point: Jesus rose from the dead so you can be sure you are forgiven!

Jesus was handed over to die for our sins. He was raised to life in order to make us right with God. (Romans 4:25, NIRV)

Can God truly forgive you? Yes, Jesus not only died for you but He rose from the dead so that you can know with certainty that His sacrifice was acceptable, your sins are forgiven, and that you can have a good relationship with God forever. This grace gives you confidence to enter into a relationship with Him...

E stands for Eternal Life

Grace point: Eternal life is a forever relationship with God that starts the moment you choose to believe!

Whoever hears my word and believes him who sent me has eternal life and will not be condemned. (John 5:24, NIV)

Because of the grace that God has extended to you, you can enjoy a personal relationship with Him forever – this is eternal life. It starts when you stop trying to live life without Him (going your own way) and turn to the LORD Jesus. This is not about rules but relationship. When you follow the LORD Jesus, He will guide you in the path you should go. Will this mean changes? Absolutely! By grace God meets you where you are and will work to transform you daily into the person He wants you to be ...

❖ Closing Points

Now that you have seen and understand God's gift of grace to you, is there any reason you would *not* want to accept God's grace?

> YET TO ALL WHO RECEIVED HIM, TO THOSE WHO BELIEVED IN HIS NAME, HE GAVE THE RIGHT TO BECOME CHILDREN OF GOD.
> (JOHN 1:12, NIV)

Will you prayerfully accept God's grace? You can be forgiven of your sins and enter into a relationship with the LORD Jesus starting right now. Here is a prayer you might pray – the specific words are not a magic formula. God knows your thoughts and considers the sincerity of your words.

Dear LORD Jesus,

Though I am a sinner, You are gracious. Thank you for forgiving my sins and giving me eternal life. I believe in You and will follow you as my LORD and Savior. Amen!

If you meant these words when you prayed to the LORD, He heard your prayer and granted you eternal life. You ARE forgiven, you ARE loved, and you ARE a child of God now. Welcome to God's family!

Be sure to go and tell as many people as you can about the wonderful GRACE that God has for everyone.

About the Author

Randy Lariscy is not a *gospel gunslinger*. Over  the years, numerous personality tests have confirmed what he knows from personal experience: he is an introvert. But he loves people and loves to see people enter into a loving relationship with the LORD Jesus. Randy is a bivocational minister working in both the business and ministry worlds. This has provided Randy with unique insights regarding sharing your faith in ways that are both practical and relevant.

His spiritual gifts and passion have concentrated his ministry work in discipleship and evangelism. His ministry roles have been varied including that of Education Pastor, Evangelism Consultant, Radio Bible Teacher, and Supply Preacher. He currently serves as Associate Pastor at GracePointe Marietta Church overseeing discipleship and outreach.

He holds a B.B.A. in Finance, M.A. in Pastoral Ministry, Master of Divinity, and Doctorate in Theology. Residing in Kennesaw, Georgia, Randy is happily married with two adult children and three grandchildren.

Quality resources with significant spiritual impact

On the web at www.WordTruthPress.Org

Look for more great resources from WordTruth Press:

 $6.99 USD	**Heaven** *Your Amazing Journey Home* Jesus gave you this amazing promise: **In my Father's house are many rooms. I go there to prepare a place for you.** What an amazing grace indeed is this place He calls Heaven. And Jesus wants you to be with Him there — He wants you to make the journey home. Heaven reveals both the present hope and incredible future for all who believe.

WORDTRUTH PRESS

 *$9.95 USD*	**Portraits of Forgiveness (2nd Ed.)** Finding the Inspiration and Courage to Forgive Like an old, frayed blanket there are many loose threads in our relationships. Issues and conflict divide us from family, friends, and innumerable people we encounter throughout life. The process of forgiveness is necessary to restore and rebuild those relationships. In this book you will find great stories of how God works in the lives of people to bring about forgiveness and reconciliation - binding up the loose threads and making relationships even stronger than before.
 $9.95 USD Qty 50	**The Ten Commandments** ***Evangelism Tract (Qty 50)*** The Ten Commandments are shown on the front of this 3x5 card with a positive version of each command. On the back is a presentation of the gospel. It is printed with a glossy, color front and black-and-white back.
 $9.95 USD Qty 50	**The Gospel of GRACE** ***Evangelism Tract (Qty 50)*** This attractive 3x5 card presents the good news using the word GRACE as an acrostic. Each letter represents a different aspect of God's grace at work in salvation. Glossy, color front and black-and-white back.

QUALITY RESOURCES WITH SIGNIFICANT SPIRITUAL IMPACT

 *Available now* *$15.95 USD*	**Speedy Devotions** ***Volume One – Wise Choices*** Do you have only a little time to study the Bible? Or does the Bible seem intimidating in its size and scope? Many find it hard to stay focused on long passages of Scripture. Yet the Bible is God's word for all people. And even a small amount of God's word can have a profound impact on your life. Volume 1 is about wise choices. This devotional takes you through the book of Proverbs where you learn great wisdom in small portions each day
 *Available now* *$9.95 USD*	**The Book of Mark** ***Volume 1: Chapters 1-6*** The Insight Bible Commentary Series (IBC) is designed with clarity in mind. Not only will you find clear explanations of what the Bible is saying but also unique insights into how you can apply God's eternal truths to daily living. The book of Mark is generally held to be the earliest account of the life of Jesus Christ. It clearly defines its purpose in the very first verse: "The beginning of the gospel about Jesus Christ, the Son of God" (Mark 1:1, NIV). From there, the narrative presents a rapid, almost urgent look at the life of Jesus Christ. He is shown to be the Son of God with great power and authority.

WordTruth Press

The mission of WordTruth Press is to provide quality Bible-based resources with significant spiritual impact for individuals and churches. Education and evangelism are the main focus of WordTruth Press. Following the Great Commission of the LORD Jesus[29] this organization provides Bible-based resources to evangelize the world, encourage and equip believers and churches for evangelism, and provide solid Bible teaching to build up the body of Christ.

A key strategy is to find low-cost channels for production and distribution to maximize the availability of our resources to people around the world. WordTruth Press also offers many free resources for churches and individuals available online at: WordTruthPress.Org

---

[29] *Matthew 28:18-20.*

www.ingramcontent.com/pod-product-compliance
Lightning Source LLC
Chambersburg PA
CBHW020005050426
42450CB00005B/318